Learning How to Control My E[motions]
Jessica Gardner, an exper[t]
specializing in student de-esc[alation]
assist students in mastering [de-]
escalation techniques. Gardner's compassionate approach underscores the significance of mental well-being and self-regulation in student development. Through practical guidance, the book challenges students to enhance their behavior by learning to regulate their emotions effectively. By offering empowering strategies and exercises, students are equipped with the necessary tools to manage stress and cultivate a composed and attentive mindset. Gardner's commitment to nurturing emotional regulation in students renders this book an invaluable asset for those seeking to improve their well-being and personal development.

Jessica Gardner's book not only provides insightful strategies for students to master relaxation and de-escalation techniques but also emphasizes the importance of mental well-being and self-regulation in their overall growth. With a compassionate and empowering approach, Gardner guides students towards enhancing their behavior by effectively managing their emotions. The practical guidance and exercises offered in the book serve as valuable tools to help students navigate stress and cultivate a calm and focused mindset. Through Gardner's dedication to fostering emotional regulation in students, this book serves as a beacon for those looking to enhance their well-being and personal development.

I am happy!

When I am happy,
I can be a good
friend.

When I am happy,
I can do my work.

When I am happy,
I can share with my friend.

When I am happy,
I can dance with my friend.

When I am happy, I can read with my friend.

I am Sad!

When I am Sad,
I can sit by myself.

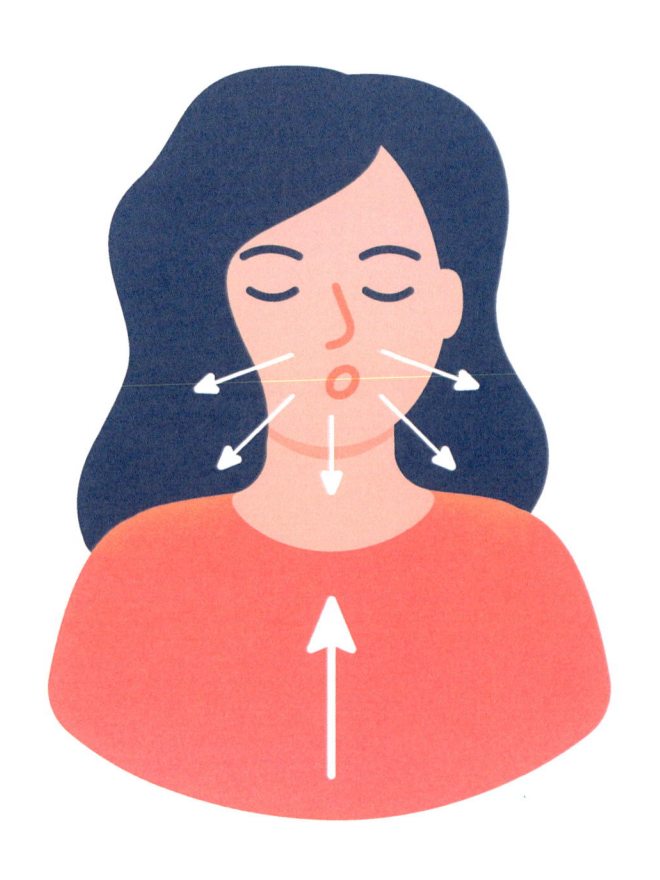

When I am Sad, I can take deep breathes.

When I am Sad,
I can read a book.

When I am Sad,
I can rest.

When I am Sad,
can watch a Video.

I am Mad!

When I am Mad, I cannot throw items.

When I am Mad,
I cannot hit friends.

When I am Mad,
I cannot hide from
adults.

When I am Mad,
I cannot tear paper

When I am Mad,
I cannot say mean
things.

When I am Mad, I cannot punch others.

I am Excited!

When I am Excited,
I can play games.

When I am Excited, I can celebrate with my friends.

When I am Excited,
I can learn
something new.

When I am Excited,
I can listen to my
Teacher.

When I am Excited,
I can help others.

I am Calm!

When I am Calm,
I can be a Leader.

When I am Calm,
I can be Kind to my friends.

When I am Calm, I can be work together with my friends.

When I am Calm,
I can be play
together with my
friends.

When I am Calm, I can be eat together with my friends.

"Learning How to Control My Emotions," authored by Jessica Gardner, delves into Social/Emotional Learning, a meticulously designed program by a committed educator with a profound interest in social-emotional development. The primary objective is to equip students with the skills to manage their emotions adeptly. This endeavor seeks to enhance the connection between educators and students, cultivating an environment conducive to learning. As I pursue an Education degree at Western Governors University, my professional journey has encompassed diverse roles. My fervor lies in supporting children to reach their academic and personal goals through collaborative efforts.

In my experience, I have discovered that fostering emotional intelligence is crucial in creating a nurturing and supportive learning environment. By understanding and managing their emotions effectively, students can navigate challenges with resilience and empathy. As I continue my education at Western Governors University, I am committed to honing my skills in social-emotional learning and implementing innovative strategies in the classroom. Together, educators and students can cultivate a community where everyone feels valued, understood, and empowered to thrive academically and personally.

Milton Keynes UK
Ingram Content Group UK Ltd.
UKRC031322260324
440148UK00005B/126